Rumi

100 LOVE POEMS & QUOTES

Take a journey

into the

Heart

Jalal al-Din Rumi
&
Imur Evol

Dedicated to all the hearts in the world

"One went to the door of the Beloved and knocked.

A voice asked: "Who is there?"

He answered: "It is I."

The voice said: "There is no room here for me and thee."

The door was shut.

After a year of solitude and deprivation

this man returned to the door of the Beloved.

He knocked.

A voice from within asked: "Who is there?"

The man said: "It is Thou."

The door was opened for him."

"If you are seeking, seek us with joy

For we live in the kingdom of joy.

Do not give your heart to anything else

But to the love of those who are clear joy,

Do not stray into the neighborhood of despair.

For there are hopes: they are real, they exist—

Do not go in the direction of darkness—

I tell you: suns exist."

"Love so needs to love

that it will endure almost anything, even abuse,

just to flicker for a moment.

But the sky's mouth is kind,

its song will never hurt you,

for I sing those words."

"Love isn't the work of the tender and the gentle;

Love is the work of wrestlers.

The one who becomes a servant of lovers

is really a fortunate sovereign.

Don't ask anyone about Love;

ask Love about Love.

Love is a cloud that scatters pearls."

"I'm in love!

Your advice, what are they?

Love has poisoned me!

Your remedies, what are they?

I hear them shout: "fast, bind his feet!"

But if my heart that has gone mad!

Those strings on my feet

What is the point?"

"You think you are alive

because you breathe air?

Shame on you,

that you are alive in such a limited way.

Don't be without Love,

so you won't feel dead.

Die in Love

and stay alive forever."

"To Love is to be God.

Never will a Lover's chest

feel any sorrow.

Never will a Lover's robe

be touched by mortals.

Never will a Lover's body

be found buried in the earth.

To Love is to be God."

"In your light I learn how to love.

In your beauty, how to make poems.

You dance inside my chest where no-one sees you,

but sometimes I do,

and that sight becomes this art."

"Believe in love's infinite journey,

for it is your own,

for you are love.

Love is life."

"I want that love that moved the mountains.

I want that love that split the ocean.

I want that love that made the winds tremble.

I want that love that roared like thunder.

I want that love that will raise the dead.

I want that love that lifts us to ecstasy.

I want that love that is the silence of eternity."

"The minute I heard my first love story,

I started looking for you, not knowing

how blind that was.

Lovers don't finally meet somewhere.

They're in each other all along."

"We are the mirror, as well as the face in it.

We are tasting the taste of eternity this minute.

We are pain and what cures pain.

We are the sweet cold water and the jar that pours.

Soul of the world, no life, nor world remain,

no beautiful women and men longing.

Only this ancient love circling

the holy black stone of nothing.

Where the lover is the loved,

the horizon and everything within it."

"The only lasting beauty is the beauty of the heart."

"My love, you are closer to me than myself

You shine through my eyes,

Your light is brighter than the Moon

Step into the garden so all the flowers

Even the tall poplar can kneel before your beauty

Let your voice silence the lily famous for its hundred tongues,

When you want to be kind

You are softer than the soul

But when you withdraw

You can be so cold and harsh.

Dear one, you can be wild and rebellious

But when you meet him face to face

His charm will make you docile like the earth,

Throw away your shield and bare your chest

There is no stronger protection than him.

That's why when the Lover withdraws from the world

He covers all the cracks in the wall

So the outside light cannot come though,

He knows that only the inner light illuminates his world!"

"Die! Die! Die in this love!

If you die in this love,

Your soul will be renewed.

Die! Die!

Don't fear the death of that which is known

If you die to the temporal,

You will become timeless."

"You call out, I am the lover,

But these are mere words.

If you see lover and Beloved as two,

you either have double vision,

or you can't count."

"Sometimes I wonder, sweetest love, if you

Were a mere dream in along winter night,

A dream of spring-days, and of golden light

Which sheds its rays upon a frozen heart;

A dream of wine that fills the drunken eye.

And so I wonder, sweetest love, if I

Should drink this ruby wine, or rather weep;

Each tear a bezel with your face engraved,

A rosary to memorize your name…

There are so many ways to call you back-

Yes, even if you only were a dream."

"A woman is a beam of the divine light

she is not the being

whom sensual desire takes as it's object

she is a creator it should be said

she is not a creature

she is infinite love."

"You come to us from another world

From beyond the stars and void of space.

Transcendent, Pure,

Of unimaginable beauty,

Bringing with you the essence of love.

You transform all who are touched by you.

Mundane concerns, troubles,

and sorrows dissolve in your presence,

Bringing joy to ruler and ruled

To peasant and King.

You bewilder us with your grace.

All evils transform into goodness.

You are the master alchemist.

You light the fire of love in earth and sky

in heart and soul of every being.

Through your loving existence and nonexistence merge.

All opposites unite.

All that is profane

becomes sacred again."

"Oh Beloved, take me.

Liberate my soul.

Fill me with your love and

release me from the two worlds.

If I set my heart on anything but you

let fire burn me from inside.

Oh Beloved, take away what I want.

Take away what I do.

Take away what I need.

Take away everything that takes me from you"

"Be drunk with Love,

for Love is all that exists.

Where is intimacy found

if not in the give and take of Love."

"My heart is burning with love,

all can see this flame.

My heart is pulsing with passion like waves on an ocean.

My friends have become strangers and

I'm surrounded by enemies,

but I'm free as the wind no longer hurt

by those who reproach me.

I'm at home wherever I am and in the room of lovers

I can see with closed eyes the beauty that dances.

Behind the veils intoxicated with love

I too dance the rhythm of this moving world.

I have lost my senses in my world of lovers."

"All through eternity

Beauty unveils His exquisite form

in the solitude of nothingness;

He holds a mirror to His Face

and beholds His own beauty.

He is the knower and the known,

the seer and the seen;

No eye but His own

has ever looked upon this Universe.

His every quality finds an expression:

Eternity becomes the verdant field of Time and Space;

Love, the life-giving garden of this world.

Every branch and leaf and fruit

Reveals an aspect of His perfection.

The cypress give hint of His majesty,

The rose gives tidings of His beauty.

Whenever Beauty looks,

Love is also there;

Whenever beauty shows a rosy cheek

Love lights Her fire from that flame.

When beauty dwells in the dark folds of night

Love comes and finds a heart

entangled in tresses.

Beauty and Love are as body and soul.

Beauty is the mine, Love is the diamond.

They have together since the beginning of time-

Side by side, step by step."

"There is a path from me to you

that I am constantly looking for."

"Love Came.... and became like blood in my body.

It rushed through my veins and encircled my Heart.

Everywhere I looked, I saw One Thing.

Love's Name written on my limbs, on my left palm,

on my forehead,

on the back of my neck,

on my right big toe.

Oh, my friend, all that you see of me is just a shell,

and the rest belongs to Love."

"Heart is a sea, language is the shore.

Whatever is in a sea hits the shore."

"When Love comes suddenly

and taps on your window, run and let it in

but first, shut the door of your reason.

Even the smallest hint chases love away

like smoke that drowns

the freshness of the morning breeze.

To reason Love can only say,

the way is barred, you can't pass through

but to the lover it offers a hundred blessings.

Before the mind decides to take a step

Love has reached the seventh heaven.

Before the mind can figure how

Love has climbed the Holy Mountain.

I must stop this talk now and let

Love speak from its nest of silence."

"Love is neither a tale nor a game.

Love is such a powerful torrent

that no one can stand in front of it.

Love is the flame which, when it blazes,

consumes everything other than the Beloved."

"If I hold you in my heart, you'll wither;

Become a thorn if I hold you in my eyes.

No, I'll make a place for you within my soul instead,

So you'll be my love in lives beyond this life."

"The beauty of the heart is the lasting beauty:

its lips give to drink of the water of life.

Truly it is the water,

that which pours,

and the one who drinks.

All three become one when

your talisman is shattered.

That oneness you can't know by reasoning."

"Love is the bridge between you and everything."

"There is a place born of silence

A place where the whispers of the heart arise.

There is a place where voices sing your beauty

A place where every breath

carves your image in my soul."

"Goodbyes are only for those who love with their eyes.

Because for those who love with heart and soul

there is no such thing as separation."

"Let the beauty of what you love be what you do."

"I am only the house of your beloved,

not the beloved herself:

true love is for the treasure,

not for the coffer that contains it.

The real beloved is that one who is unique,

who is your beginning and your end.

When you find that one,

you'll no longer expect anything else:

that is both the manifest and the mystery.

That one is the lord of states of feeling,

dependent on none;

month and year are slaves to that moon.

When he bids the "state,"

it does His bidding;

when that one wills, bodies become spirit."

"The springtime of Lovers has come,

that this dust bowl may become a garden;

the proclamation of heaven has come,

that the bird of the soul may rise in flight.

The sea becomes full of pearls,

the salt marsh becomes sweet as kauthar,

the stone becomes a ruby from the mine,

the body becomes wholly soul."

"It is Love and the Lover that live eternally -

Don't lend your heart to anything else;

all else is borrowed."

"I said: what about my eyes?

He said: Keep them on the road.

I said: What about my passion?

He said: Keep it burning.

I said: What about my heart?

He said: Tell me what you hold inside it?

I said: Pain and sorrow.

He said: Stay with it.

The wound is the place

Where the Light enters you."

"In the realm of lovers

There is only one beloved

In this realm of lovers

There is no coming nor going

Lovers wander

Looking for each other

There is no need for this wandering

The soul of Lovers lives in a place beyond time

The one beloved

Searching for herself in the other

Let us become passionate lovers

Lovers in life

Lovers in death

Lovers in the tomb

Lovers on the day of resurrection

Lovers in paradise

Lovers forever

If you have not known this love don't count your life as lived

On the Day of Judgment it will not be counted

There is a bazaar

Where love is traded for free

There is a river of wine

Where drunken merriment knows no rest

Where burning passion knows no repose

Where billions of galaxies dance

Where restless lovemaking

Gives birth to Universe upon Universe."

"What you seek is seeking you."

"I am a sculptor, a molder of form.

In every moment I shape an idol.

But then, in front of you, I melt them down.

I can rouse a hundred forms

and fill them with spirit,

but when I look into your face,

I want to throw them in the fire.

My souls spills into yours and is blended.

Because my soul has absorbed your fragrance,

I cherish it.

Every drop of blood I spill

informs the earth,

I merge with my Beloved

when I participate in love.

In this house of mud and water,

my heart has fallen to ruins.

Enter this house, my Love, or let me leave."

"This is love:

to fly toward a secret sky,

to cause a hundred veils to fall each moment.

First, to let go of life.

In the end, to take a step without feet;

to regard this world as invisible,

and to disregard what appears to be the self.

Heart, I said, what a gift it has been

to enter this circle of lovers,

to see beyond seeing itself,

to reach and feel within the breast."

"Should everything pass away,

it couldn't happen without You.

This heart of mines bears Your imprint;

it has nowhere else to turn.

The eye of the intellect is drunk with You,

the wheeling galaxy is humble before You,

the ear of ecstasy is in Your hand;

nothing happens without You.

The soul is bubbling with You,

the heart imbibes from You,

the intellect bellows in rapture;

nothing happens without You.

You, my grape wine and my intoxication,

my rose garden and my springtime,

my sleep and repose;

nothing happens without You.

You are my grandeur and glory,

you are my possessions and prosperity,

you are my purest water;

nothing happens without You"

This is the prayer of each:

You are the source of my life.

You separate essence from mud.

You honor my soul.

You bring rivers from the mountain springs.

You brighten my eyes.

The wine you offer takes me out of myself

into the self we share.

Doing that is religion."

"Your task is not to seek for love,

but merely to seek and find all the barriers

within yourself that you have built against it."

"The garden of love is green

without limit and yields

many fruits other than sorrow or joy.

Love is beyond either condition:

without spring, without autumn, it is always fresh."

"When I am with you, we stay up all night.

When you're not here, I can't go to sleep.

Praise God for those two insomnias!

And the difference between them."

"If the house of the world is dark,

Love will find a way to create windows."

"I swear, since seeing Your face,

the whole world is fraud and fantasy

The garden is bewildered as to what is leaf or blossom.

The distracted birds can't distinguish

the birdseed from the snare.

A house of love with no limits,

a presence more beautiful than venus or the moon,

a beauty whose image fills the mirror of the heart."

"Let yourself be drawn by the stronger pull

of that which you truly love."

"Love is a river. Drink from it."

"O lovers, lovers it is time

to set out from the world.

I hear a drum in my soul's ear

coming from the depths of the stars.

Our camel driver is at work;

the caravan is being readied.

He asks that we forgive him

for the disturbance he has caused us,

He asks why we travelers are asleep.

Everywhere the murmur of departure;

the stars, like candles

thrust at us from behind blue veils,

and as if to make the invisible plain,

a wondrous people have come forth."

"If destiny comes to help you,

Love will come to meet you.

A life without love isn't a life."

"Come on sweetheart

let's adore one another

before there is no more of you and me."

"The time has come to turn

your heart into a temple of fire.

Your essence is gold hidden in dust.

To reveal its splendor

you need to burn in the fire of love."

"Love is the whole thing. We are only pieces."

"May this marriage be blessed.

May this marriage be as sweet as milk and honey.

May this marriage be as intoxicating as old wine.

May this marriage be fruitful like a date tree.

May this marriage be full of laughter

and everyday a paradise.

May this marriage be a seal of compassion

for here and hereafter.

May this marriage be as welcome

as the full moon in the night sky.

Listen lovers, now you go on,

as I become silent and kiss this blessed night."

"When you seek Love with all your Heart,

you shall find its echoes in the universe."

"A lover asked his beloved,

Do you love yourself more than you love me?

Beloved replied,

I have died to myself and I live for you.

I've disappeared from myself and my attributes,

I am present only for you.

I've forgotten all my learnings,

but from knowing you I've become a scholar.

I've lost all my strength,

but from your power I am able.

I love myself...I love you.

I love you...I love myself."

"To Love is to reach God."

"Reason is powerless in the expression of Love.

Love alone is capable of revealing the truth of

Love and being a Lover.

The way of our prophets is the way of Truth.

If you want to live, die in Love;

die in Love if you want to remain alive."

"Love is the sea where intellect drowns."

"You live in my heart where

no one sees you but I do.

That vision becomes this art."

"Love is the cure,

for your pain will keep giving birth

to more pain until

your eyes constantly exhale love

as effortlessly as your body yields its scent."

I want to see you.

Know your voice.

Recognize you when you

first come 'round the corner.

Sense your scent when I come

into a room you've just left.

Know the lift of your heel,

the glide of your foot.

Become familiar with the way

you purse your lips

then let them part,

just the slightest bit,

when I lean in to your space and kiss you.

I want to know the joy of how you whisper

"More"

"Come out of the circle of time

And into the circle of love."

"Love has nothing to do with

the five senses and the six directions:

its goal is only to experience

the attraction exerted by the Beloved.

Afterwards, perhaps, permission

will come from God:

the secrets that ought to be told with be told

with an eloquence nearer to the understanding

that these subtle confusing allusions.

The secret is partner with none

but the knower of the secret:

in the skeptic's ear the secret is no secret at all."

"The mirror of the heart must be clear,

so you can discern the ugly from the beautiful."

"Be wild and crazy and drunk with Love,

if you are too careful,

LOVE will not find you."

"Look at Love... how it tangles with the one fallen in love ."

"One day

You will take my heart completely

and make it more fiery than a dragon.

Your eyelashes will write on my heart

the poem that could never come

from the pen of a poet."

"Let yourself be silently drawn

by the strange pull

of what you really love.

It will not lead you astray."

"Listen!

Clam up your mouth and be silent like an oyster shell,

for that tongue of yours is the enemy of the soul, my friend.

When the lips are silent,

the heart has a hundred tongues."

"Outside ideas of right doing and wrong doing, there is a field.

I'll meet you there."

"Be certain that in the religion of Love

there are no believers and unbelievers.

LOVE embraces all."

"If you have not learned to be a passionate lover,

do not count your life as lived.

On the day of reckoning, it will not be counted."

"My longing for you keeps me in this moment

My passion gives me courage."

"Love possesses seven hundred wings, and each one

extends from the highest heaven to the lowest earth."

"Reason is powerless in the expression of Love."

"Only from the heart can you touch the sky."

"The garden of the world has no limits except in your mind.

Its presence is more beautiful than the stars with more clarity

than the polished mirror of your heart."

"Plant the love of the holy ones within your spirit;

don't give your heart to anything,

but the love of those whose hearts are glad."

"You have to keep breaking your heart until it opens."

"I love my friends

neither with my heart nor with my mind.

Just in case…

Heart might stop.

Mind can forget.

I love them with my soul.

Soul never stops or forgets."

"One day your heart will take you to your Lover.

One day your soul will carry you to the Beloved.

Don't get lost in your pain,

know that one day your pain will become your cure."

"The heart is like a candle

longing to be lit.

Torn from the beloved

it yearns to be whole again,

but you have to bear the pain.

You cannot learn about love.

Love appears on the wings of grace."

"Gamble everything for love, if you're a true human being."

"Love is from the infinite, and will remain until eternity.

The seeker of love escapes the chains of birth and death.

Tomorrow, when resurrection comes,

The heart that is not in love will fail the test."

"Love is a mirror.

In it you see nothing except your reflection.

You see nothing except your real face."

"Love is language that cannot be said, or heard."

"Love is not written on paper, for paper can be erased.

Nor is it etched on stone, for stone can be broken.

But it is inscribed on a heart and there it shall remain forever."

"Love is our steady guide on this road full of hardships."

"We are born of love. Love is our mother."

"I merged so completely with love,

and was so fused,

that I became Love and Love became me."

"The heart is your student, for love is the only way we learn."

Made in the USA
Coppell, TX
04 January 2021

47556961R00060